Two stone pillars, or 'The Pylons' as they are known, stand proud at the northern entrance to the city on the A23, welcoming drivers. Erected in 1928, the foundation stones were laid by the Duke and Duchess of York (later King George VI and the Queen Mother). Narrowly avoiding demolition when the A23 was widened in the early 1990s, the Pylons have now become firm fixtures, a friendly sight at Brighton's borders.

Local newspapers and artefacts from 1928 are buried inside the Pylons, including the inscription:
'Hail guest, we ask not what thou art. If friend, we greet thee hand and heart. If stranger, no longer be. If foe, our love shall conquer thee.'
Welcome, then, to Brighton and Hove.

Brighton History

The name Brighton is derived from the Old English *Beorhthelmes tūn*, meaning Beorhthelm's farmstead. It went through a number of derivatives thereafter, settling on Brighthelmston by the 19th century before being shortened yet further. There is evidence of habitation in the area from Neolithic times onwards, and a brief mention of local settlements in the Norman 'Domesday Book' census of 1086, but it is not until 1514 that the first clear illustration of the town is recorded - an annotated map recording how it had recently been burnt down by French raiders.

By 1640, Brighthelmstone (as it was then spelled) had developed into a busy fishing community, with over 4000 inhabitants, but hardship and a series of storms that destroyed coastal structures saw economic decline and a severe fall in population by the mid-18th century. In a twist of fate, however, one that would determine a better future for the town, a health fad for the drinking of seawater in the 1700s saw a series of doctors draw particular attention to the (supposedly) beneficial effects of the local source. Soon, the gentle folk of England were travelling to Brighthelmston in their thousands, encouraged by the happy patronage of the Prince Regent, who turned a farmhouse retreat into the gloriously eccentric stylings of the Royal Pavilion.

The coming of the railways and the new enthusiasm for seaside holidays in the 1800s saw the building of hotels, beach huts and piers, and the now-foreshortened Brighton became the place it is today.

Surviving 56 bombing raids and 198 fatalities during the course of the Second World War, the town began to flourish again in the post-austerity years. A brief decline in the 1970s and 80s, which saw the town lose some of its sheen, was happily reversed in later decades, crowned with Brighton's vital elevation to the status of city in 2000, officially unified with neighbouring Hove at last. Now it is a major cultural vortex, as well as a sporting one, hosting as it does the Sussex County Cricket Club, Brighton & Hove Albion Football Club, Brighton Racecourse and a greyhound racing circuit amongst many other activities (all beyond the remit of this book). Few want for things to do in Brighton.

A strong artistic and performing community resides in the city, along with a keen presence of students from both Brighton and Sussex Universities and a notable contingent of Britain's gay and lesbian population. All are drawn by a feeling of inclusiveness and a can-do attitude that seems to seep up from its pavements and offer opportunity to those with initiative and ambition, as the Prince Regent showed.

One: Brighton Seafront

The Seafront

When visitors think of Brighton, it is very often the distinctive and bustling seafront that they picture in their minds. So where better to start a pictorial guide than by exploring the colourful sights and atmosphere of the most familiar aspect of this lively and iconic seaside resort. It was the Victorians that actively moulded Brighton into first a health spa and then a major holiday hotspot, and it has retained its broad appeal ever since.

On a sunny summer weekend or Bank Holiday, thousands flock to Brighton and Hove to enjoy the busy seafront cafes and promenade walks, with their unique architecture and panoramic views of the English Channel. Traditional novelty shops (including purveyors of the famous 'Brighton rock', of course) vie for space in alcoves and arches with sophisticated art galleries, bars and trendy clubs.

It is not just visitors who come to enjoy the seafront. Brighton is far more than just a holiday resort and its many passionately loyal residents and workers are just as likely to be found sunning themselves here in their lunchbreaks and days off.

Seafront Life

Trinkets, stickers and saucy postcards are staple components of seaside life and all are present and correct along the front.

Excellent sports facilities and acrobatic amusements make for a constantly busy seafront at all times in summer daylight hours, with every age and taste well-catered for.

Early evening brings a new atmosphere to the seafront (seen here at Hove) as colours fill the sky, cyclists and joggers home from work emerge for their evening exercise routines, and couples stroll romantically. Meanwhile, others inhabit shelters to enjoy the last golden glow of the sun and indulge in the gossip of the day.

Designed by sculptor Bruce Williams as a 'celebration... calling for equality, understanding and acceptance', Kiss Wall *was installed in 1992.*

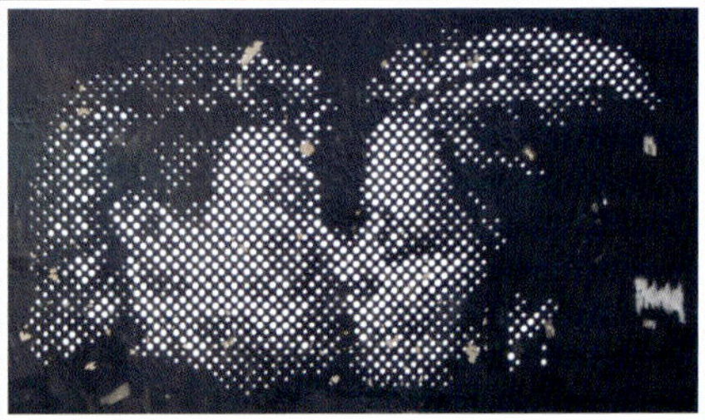

The seafront is home to some distinctive art which, despite the best efforts of the elements and vandals, still maintain a dignity and presence. The unique 'kissing monument', made from holes drilled into cast-iron, remains a favourite of many, summing up the romantic and all-lifestyle-inclusive side of the Brightonian spirit.

A work of art in its own right, the Brighton Bandstand, or 'Birdcage' as it is sometimes known, was first constructed in 1884 as a shelter for Victorian ladies near the West Pier (pages 14-15), but quickly became an ideal facility for music and events. It fell into sad decay (below) from the 1970s onwards, but a keen campaign happily saw it reopen in its full glory as a cafe and venue in 2009.

The Pier

The one remaining active pier first opened in 1899 and originally contained a concert hall for more highbrow events than we might expect today. Now unashamedly garish and commercial, it is everything seaside life is expected to be and enjoys masses of visitors each year. Known for many years as the Palace Pier (to distinguish it from the earlier West Pier), the demise of its rival (pages 14-15) enabled what is now the central draw for seafront amusement-seekers to rename itself simply 'Brighton Pier' in 2000.

The distinctive glitter ball weathervane can often be seen catching the sunlight from long distances on bright days.

Brighton Pier is the current survivor of three. The first, the Royal Suspension Chain Pier, was an elegant and quite different prospect to today's construction. Built in 1823, it fell into disrepair (rather like the West Pier) and was finally destroyed by a storm in 1896. The Palace Pier was its replacement, retaining some of the original entrance kiosks and its signal cannon. Low tides occasionally reveal a few remaining iron piles from the foundations of the old Chain Pier to fascinate those with an eye for history.

Pier Life

The Palace Pier has become an iconic presence in screen fiction over the years, in everything from *Carry-On* movies to *Oh! What a Lovely War* and the famously sinister ghost train scene in the 1947 adaptation of Graham Greene's novel *Brighton Rock*. The huge funfair at its far end has now expanded to incorporate everything from roller coasters, log flumes and helter-skelters to the traditional win-a-prize kiosks and amusement arcades. Larger events are occasionally mounted, such as a hugely successful *Doctor Who* exhibition in 2005 to celebrate the then newly-revived sci-fi television series.

A serious overnight fire destroyed some of the funfair in 2003, but a quick rebuild and new safety regulations saw the pier quickly recover to retake its place as the seafront's biggest attraction.

The pier is a draw for people of all ages and visited all year round, as these scenes of pier life show. The smell of the sea and fish and chips must also be imagined for the full effect.

The West Pier

Built in 1866, the West Pier was another example of ornate Victorian grandeur, on the border between Brighton and Hove, and enjoyed a healthy rivalry with the Palace Pier for many years. By 1975, however, the West Pier had been allowed to deteriorate to the point where closure became necessary for safety reasons, as it awaited restoration. That restoration never came, and a succession of storms and probable arsonist fires have left the West Pier, sadly, something of a local embarrasment. Although some original components have been saved and are safely stored elsewhere, so little of the main infrastructure remains that despite it being one of only two 'Grade 1 listed' piers in Britain, the cost of what will now be a virtual rebuild has so far prevented its resurrection.

A little hope for the West Pier still remains as part of a general regeneration scheme for this part of the seafront, to be crowned with the anticipated construction of the 'i360' tower, a proposed 150 metre-high observation deck to stand almost where the original pier began. The tower will give extraordinary views of Brighton.

The sad, yet somehow evocative, remains of the West Pier still await their ultimate fate, but as each year goes by the task of 'restoration' becomes ever-more daunting.

The Beach

Sand is a rare commodity on Brighton beach, but what it lacks in softness it makes up for with character. A happy, lively atmosphere always pervades on calm summer days, and partying groups (below) and impromptu barbeques give it something of a Riviera spirit, tapped into massively by superstar DJ Fatboy Slim, whose occasional beach gigs attract thousands to the shore for the ultimate 'raves'.

Bronzed bodies lie happily alongside the traditional deck chair culture as people take from the beach whatever experience they need. For those requiring the ultimate exposure, the nudist beach at Black Rock provides the chance to throw everything off!

Volk's Electric Railway

'Volk's Electric Railway', or just 'the Volks' to locals, holds the distinction of being the 'world's oldest operating electric railway'. Founded in 1883 by inventor Magnus Volk, the line, which runs from the Palace Pier to Black Rock (which now services the Marina - pages 20-23), was a magnificent curiosity to Victorian holidaymakers and still maintains its fascination for visitors today, albeit as something of more nostalgic interest. Yet being taken effortlessly from A to B and back again, with sea views, seems to hold eternal appeal.

Volk's Railway has seen many changes over the years, with both extensions and removals of tracks. A viaduct once even went out over the sea, although this was not as ambitious as the 'Daddy Long Legs' train, also founded by Volks, which ran to Rottingdean on tall legs through the actual waves between 1896-1902. The current line's continuation is a welcome reminder of former times, 'the Volks' somehow having survived recessions, wars and bureacracy to remain with us today.

The Marina

Boats come and go, passing dredgers clearing the harbour entrance in what is claimed to be Europe's largest and busiest marina.

Brighton Marina began construction in 1971 and was finally opened for business by the Queen in 1978. At first a purely maritime enterprise to provide a much-needed harbour in an area lacking natural protection from the elements, the Marina has grown over the decades to encompass shops, cinemas and restaurants, with its own large residential community.

Expensive yachts and smaller vessels mingle with fishing boats at the Marina. Despite Brighton's original heritage as a fishing village, it wasn't until the Marina arrived that proper facilities were made available to those who earn their livelihoods from the sea.

Marina Residential

The blocks of luxury apartments that have grown up around the Marina over the years have made the area a village in its own right. Visitors, meanwhile, enjoy strolling the boardwalks and taking the long hike along the harbour wall.

The Marina covers 126 acres, has over 800 separate properties, and berths an astonishing 1600 yachts and boats, whilst hosting eateries, entertainments and bars.

The Marina has become a little world of its own for both the human and non-human inhabitants of its waterways.

Looking west along Madeira Drive from Black Rock towards the city. The Drive is used for many big events (often involving cars - see pages 76-79). Clubs and bars nestle beneath the long underwalks (inset), but there are major plans for a regeneration of the area, including the building of a new sports arena and ice rinks.

Two: Brighton Life

A Busy City

The breathtaking sea of rooftops that can be viewed from various vantage points (here looking east to Brighton General Hospital - once the Victorian workhouse, which loomed ominously over the populace) reveals the vast extent of Brighton.

Barely a warm day goes by without a mass of visitors and residents appearing to soak up the atmosphere in the heart of the city (here at the Pavilion Gardens). There is always a go-ahead and positive feel in the air.

The Centre

The hub of everyday Brighton life is the Churchill Square shopping complex, an ultra-modern arcade uneasily facing architecturally interesting, if slightly tired, art-deco blocks from earlier times in Western Road. The 1998 Churchill Square replaced the previous outdoor 1960s version (unceremoniously crowned with office blocks), and now contains over 80 mainstream shops and cafes on three floors, with a vast underground car park. It may not be the most sophisticated part of the Brighton consumer experience (for that, see The Lanes, pages 32-33), but it is usually the first port of call for those seeking basics, buses or retail therapy.

For most, the very centre of Brighton is defined by the ornate and recently restored Clock Tower that first greets visitors walking down Queen's Road from the railway station (pages 40-41). Built to commemorate Queen Victoria's Golden Jubilee in 1887, it is adorned at its base with statues and mosaics of Victoria, Prince Albert and the then Prince and Princess of Wales. The crowning golden sphere elegantly rises and falls to mark each hour.

The original golden sphere mechanism, long-dormant but now working again, was devised by Magnus Volk, who also founded the electric seafront railway (pages 18-19).

Churchill Square

Shopping arcades, old and new, in and around Churchill Square. Brighton has long been a prosperous and thriving town, even in harder times.

Imperial Arcade, just off Western Road.

The internal centre of Churchill Square.

The cathedral-like inside of Churchill Square, the primary centre of the shopping experience in Brighton.

The Lanes

Goods aren't cheap in The Lanes, but people are happy to pay for exclusivity and a unique shopping experience. The passageways can become very crowded on busy days, but one learns to negotiate the sandwich boards and buskers - all part of the Lanes experience.

'The Lanes', today a labyrinth of fascinating independent shops amongst narrow walkways, have emerged from the remains of the original fishing village that grew into modern Brighton.

An outdoor cafe and fountain awaits in the square at the centre of The Lanes (above), where the architecture is rather more 1960s than most of the 18th century layout around it.

North Laines

Another area to seek out for a unusual shopping adventure is Kensington Gardens and the surrounding streets, known as the North Laines (in the blocks east of Queens Road). Considered by many to be the more alternative 'Boho' (Bohemian) centre of Brighton, these less upmarket but fascinating lanes are full of unusual retailers, street traders, risqué clothing emporiums and Tardis-like bric-a-brac/ antique centres with endless connecting rooms.

On summer days, Gardner Street, just off the North Laines, becomes one massive street cafe and market place. There is always a feeling of uplift and a relaxed atmosphere.

Street Life

Outdoor culture comes to the fore in a big way on warm summer days, with increased pedestrianisation (as here at New Road) having opened up many parts of Brighton to a cleaner, safer and friendlier way of life in more recent years.

Another busy scene of outdoor cafes and bustling activity, here at Duke Street. Buskers are also another familiar site on many of Brighton's streets any day of the year.

Every Saturday, continuing a tradition that has been running for nearly a century now, Upper Gardner Street loses its traffic and becomes a market place for stalls and traders who ply their wares to strollers hoping to pick up a bargain.

Three: Brighton Places

The Railway Station

The arrival of the railways was the making of Brighton once its line connected to London around 1840, making it the closest available seaside resort for both holidaying workers and gentle folk, bringing them in by their thousands in the days before the car. The grand scale of the station we see today befits its continued importance. The structure has developed in stages, its sweeping glass roof (recently restored) being installed in 1883 along with its classic detailed frontage.

Brighton station provides a crucial link between services to both the east and west, and up to London and beyond. Many local residents commute daily to London.

Brighton Centre and The Grand

An eyesore to some, a crucial major venue to others, when the Brighton Centre was opened in 1977 it was state of the art. Now, with its grey concrete frontage looking rather dated, and its facilities requiring expansion, there is talk of replacing it with something for new times. Yet it remains an important focal point for music, arts and sports events and is still used by major political parties for annual conferences. Delegates often stay at the directly neighbouring Grand Hotel (opposite), a plush and respected hostelry that became briefly infamous as the appalling scene of the 1984 IRA bomb that attempted to wipe out Margaret Thatcher and her cabinet.

GRAND
43

Cinemas Old and New

Directly adjacent to the Brighton Centre (page 42), the building originally known as the Kingswest complex was opened in 1972 and remains equally controversial as a piece of architecture, with its spiky top. Internally modernised over the years and externally redecorated of late, it is home to Odeon multiplex screens, and nightclubs.

The Can-Can legs (originally from an Oxford theatre production) bizarrely protruding from the roof above the bar balcony at the Duke of York's cinema have become something of a trademark. 'The Dukes' is popular with Brighton's alternative arts community.

At the other end of the cinematic spectrum, Brighton is also home to the Duke of York's (near Preston Circus), Britain's oldest continually-operating cinema, which first opened in 1910.

The Duke of York's cinema has undergone various refits, but still retains the character of yesteryear, with its single screen and unique illuminated proscenium arch. Renowned for its welcome exposure of 'arthouse' movies, the much-cherished Duke's also plays host to live opera screenings, film lectures and high-definition broadcasts of the annual Eurovision Song Contest in a riotous party mood.

The Dome

Originally the stable building for the Prince Regent's Pavilion (pages 48-51), what has become known as 'The Dome' was converted to a concert hall as early as 1860 and has gone on to become a key venue of South-East England, now also encompassing the Corn Exchange and Pavilion Theatre as part of the same complex. Most famously, it was here that pop group ABBA won the Eurovision Song Contest in 1974 with their song *Waterloo*, but it is also the place where, in 1972, Pink Floyd first attempted an entire live performance of what would become their classic album *Dark Side of the Moon*, although a technical hitch ignomiously ended it halfway through.

The entrance gate to the Pavilion gardens, directly adjacent to The Dome.

Next to The Dome, the Pavilion gardens are a popular gathering place throughout the summer months, the little cafe forever kept busy as visitors arrive to view the gargantuan wonder before them...

The Royal Pavilion

Drawn by the then claimed curative properties of seawater, the colourful and controversial Prince Regent (later King George IV) hired a farmhouse in Old Steine in 1786, and it developed somewhat from there... into Brighton's grandest structure.

Becoming known as the Royal Pavilion, a major redesign by John Nash between 1815-1822 saw the site's transformation into an exotic eastern-style palace.

Taking its initial flavour from Indian architecture, greatly in vogue as the British Empire reached its heights, in fact the dream palace of the Prince Regent is a complex mish-mash of diverse styles, incorporating everything from Islamic art on the outside to Chinese affectations in its richly-decorated interior. Appropriately, the building was called into service to house wounded Indian and West Indian servicemen in the First World War, some of whom, coming back to consciousness, believed they must have gone to heaven!

Pavilion 2

When George IV died in 1830, the Pavilion continued to be used as a recreational retreat by King William IV, but it later fell into disfavour with Queen Victoria and was sold to the town in 1850, serving as public assembly rooms for a time. The 20th century saw a programme of restoration, which has recreated its original eccentric splendour, inside and out, and it is now one of Brighton's most important and impressive attractions. (See also page 84.)

Not everybody welcomed the arrival of the Pavilion. The diarist John Wilson Croker wrote at the time: 'It is, I think, an absurd waste of money, and will be a ruin in half a century.' It has escaped his prophecy so far.

The Level & Old Steine

Created in Regency times, The Level is a vast open space surrounded by avenues of now rare Dutch and English elms, making for beautiful leafy walks. Fairgrounds, circuses and all manner of events are held on the greens throughout the year, and a playground and skateboard park keep it eternally busy. The great storm of 1987 tragically destroyed many of the older trees, but The Level has since recovered some of its former glories.

Designed in the style of a Roman water garden, the Brighton War Memorial near the Pavilion in Old Steine was designed by Sir John Simpson and erected in 1922 to commemorate the losses of around 2,600 Brightonians who fell in the First World War

The Floral Clock

Floral clocks were an affectation of the early 20th century, now lost in many towns, but the twin-faced installation (the north clock seen here) in Palmeria Square, Hove, is still maintained around the year and kept replenished with seasonal plants.

George Street in Hove has long been the central hub of activity in Hove, and since its welcome pedestrianisation in the late 1990s it is now a continually bustling and upbeat place of street cafes, farmers' markets and entertainments.

Brighton Streets

The integral warren-like terraced streets covering the eastern and western slopes of Brighton and other parts of the city (Hove, above right) have been spruced up in recent decades and now sport colourful or gleaming frontages.

The banks of houses spreading out across the downs have a beauty of their own and impressive vistas can be seen from some vantage points, such as here at Richmond Road.

Regency Style

Brunswick Square, Hove, just one of several impressive Regency-style open spaces surrounded by tall buildings adjacent to the seafront. Many of the blocks are now split into apartments, and their ocean views are much in demand.

Much of the elegant city we see today was designed in the 18th century boom that began with the arrival of the Prince Regent (page 48). The style has been adopted in much of the architecture since, with bold terraces and vast 'squares'.

Ballustrades and railings encompass some of the greens and parks in the middle of the squares, some of which are open to the public, while others (Sussex Square, main picture) are for residents only.

Art Old & New

Brighton is full of artworks, from classic statues (above right, with Queen Victoria overlooking Grand Parade in Hove, and the Edward VII 'peace statue' memorial nearby) to modern sculptures and exhibits (below, with the Sea Life Centre's 'Nautilus' submarine to the right). George IV (aka the Prince Regent, main picture), as a strong patron of the arts, would have been proud of the city's artistic reputation today.

Local comedian Max Miller is remembered outside the Dome (above), while other modern artworks pepper the city, some official, others less so, with street artist Banksy also having paid a visit (just off Trafalgar Street, above right)...

Places of Worship

There are many churches and other places of worship in Brighton and Hove, of which these are just a small selection, but several are imposing and significant as pieces of architecture. St George's in Kemptown (main picture) was commissioned by the area's founder Sir Thomas Read Kemp in 1824, and services were attended for several years by Queen Adelaide, consort of King William IV. The church is also a popular venue for events, as is the Friend's Meeting House (below) in Ship Street.

St Bartholomew's in Ann Street is claimed to be the tallest church in Britain (excluding spires). Opened in 1874, its vast space inside (opposite lower left) is certainly impressive, and its acoustics make it an excellent setting for concerts.

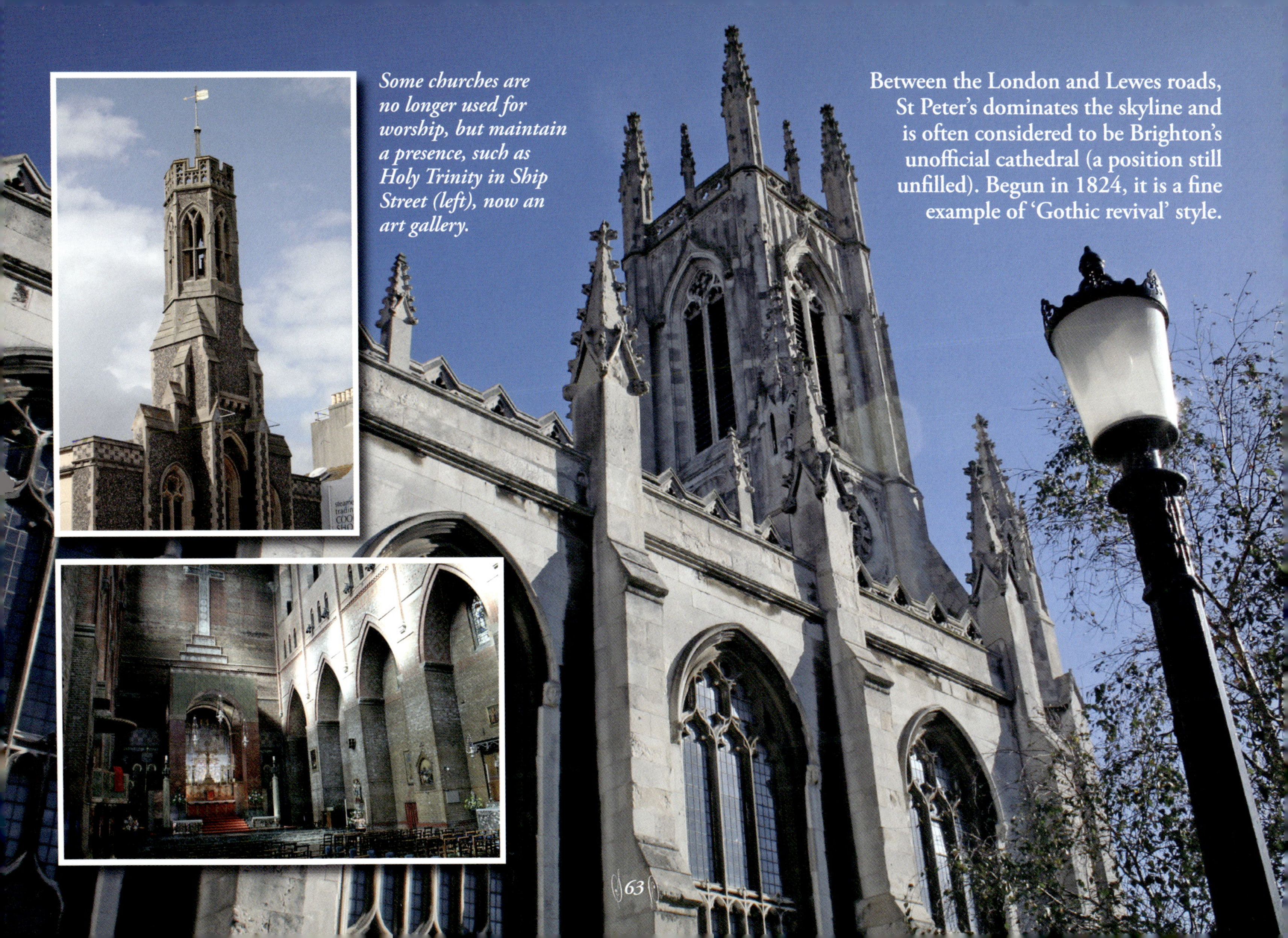

Some churches are no longer used for worship, but maintain a presence, such as Holy Trinity in Ship Street (left), now an art gallery.

Between the London and Lewes roads, St Peter's dominates the skyline and is often considered to be Brighton's unofficial cathedral (a position still unfilled). Begun in 1824, it is a fine example of 'Gothic revival' style.

Royal Sussex & Roedean

Love them or hate them, hospitals are a large part of community life and the Royal Sussex County Hospital in Kemptown is an imposing block first built in 1826 (inset, designed by Charles Barry, who went on to create the Houses of Parliament) and added to many times since. Since 2007 the buildings have been overlooked by the new Royal Alexandra wing (left of main picture), the children's hospital.

Perched on cliffs overlooking the beaches east of the Marina, Roedean School is one of the most famous educational establishments in Britain - and one of the most expensive. Situated here since 1898, the girl's boarding school has an illustrious reputation and has produced many famous pupils and members of high society. The buildings were temporarily comandeered by the Admirality during the Second World War.

A whole book could be filled with the many eclectic and atmospheric pubs and night clubs of Brighton, but this tiny collection gives an idea of the diverse mixture of architectural styles to be found, from Gothic to pop-art. The Marlborough in Princes Street, meanwhile (right), houses a tiny but popular Victorian theatre above its bar room.

Four: Brighton Events

Brighton Festival

Founded in 1966, the annual Brighton Festival attracts thousands of visitors to the city each spring with an astonishing mix of arts, performances and literary events. For several years, its most visible presence was the 'Udderbelly' tent...

The Brighton Festival is now the biggest 'multi-arts' event in England and has put the city firmly on the cultural map.

The Victoria Fountain in Old Steine, erected in 1846, is usually surrounded by event tents during the festival. The fountain is built on ancient sarsen stones found at the site, where perhaps older festivities once took place.

Some local events are rather less cultural, but keep children amused, such as this promotional comedy wrestling event held in Churchill Square..!

Festival events are held in many venues across Brighton, but the accompanying 'Fringe' festival has also blossomed in recent years and grown far beyond predictable environments. Even houses open up their living rooms to be used as art galleries - and theatres.

Children's Parade

A major part of the Brighton Festival is the now annual Children's Parade, prepared months in advance by schools, playgroups and communities around the district and finally held on a Saturday morning. Around 4000 children, teachers and parents participate in a colourful procession that can take nearly an hour to pass.

Around 10,000 people come out to watch the Children's Parade each year and enjoy the spectacle of floats, dancers, giant puppets and fledgling circus skills.

Pride Festival

Beginning as a modest event in 1992 to celebrate gay, lesbian, bisexual and transgender equality, the Brighton Pride summer festival has become the biggest annual happening of its kind in Britain and attracts many thousands of visitors.

A huge parade of floats, dancers, entertainers and revellers makes its way through the town to the main festival site at Preston Park, with music and merriment.

A huge fairground awaits the Pride parade, covering the entire expanse of Preston Park. Each year 40,000 or so local participants are joined by around 150,000 visitors, many of whom are firmly heterosexual but come along to join in the festivities and enjoy the anything-goes air of inclusivity and light-hearted freedom of expression.

Pride 2

The Pride Festival sees participants from all walks of life (the Gay Police Association, for instance, above), and spectators from old to young. Inevitably, Pride also stirs feelings from those with religious objections, who make their views very clear with boards and banners quoting biblical scripture (protest at the Clock Tower, right). With the largest gay community in Britain, Brighton can be a city of polarities, but overall it is widely recognised for its embracing and acceptance of all lifestyles and political views.

A registered charity, the Pride organisation has undergone funding and administration difficulties at times, but the main summer event (there are smaller Pride dates throughout the year) seems set to remain a major part of the Brighton calendar in one form or another.

Veteran Car Run

The London to Brighton Veteran Car Run was first staged in 1896 using cars that were then contemporary! Launched again in 1927 and held most years since (barring war or crisis), the arrival of those vintage automobiles that manage to survive the full run is now eagerly awaited each year on the first Sunday of November. Only cars made before 1905 are permitted to 'race', although in truth no record is kept of the order of arrival - finishing at all is considered achievement enough in itself.

The official finishing point for the Veteran Car Run is in Preston Park, but most vehicles then process to the seafront road of Madeira Drive where large crowds of spectators wait to see the cars arrive. The race is run in sun or rain with no mercy shown to those in the open-top carriages (most of them, in fact - these images are from a kind weather year).

Veteran Car Run 2

The city mayor greets the drivers of the wide variety of vehicles as they queue for their final destination in Madeira Drive. Television and radio celebrities, together with royalty and other dignitaries, can often be found onboard.

People line the walkways and balconies of Madeira Drive to watch the vehicles come in. Drivers of other (disallowed) vintage and classic cars will often join the run between London and Brighton too, enjoying the attention of spectators - but they don't make it into the official enclosure. The magic of archaic transport, as with the nearby Volk's Railway (pages 18-19) maintains its draw on road as well as rail.

Burning the Clocks

In 1993, a new local tradition was born, as the 'Burning of the Clocks' was initiated. Each Winter Solstice, December 21st, is now marked by the parading of elaborate lanterns representing the march of time and its annual renewal, as the days begin to lengthen again. The 'clocks' are then stacked up for a fiery demise and a fireworks celebration on the beach east of Brighton Pier.

Thousands brave the cold to attend the parade and fires, with clever costumes and ever-more ambitious constructions each year.

Five:
Brighton by Night

Night Life

With the light fading in the dusky sky, a new side of Brighton comes to life as illuminations spring up and people come into town or head out from accommodation (Grand Hotel, far right) to bars, clubs, cinemas and theatres. The Theatre Royal (right) in New Road is the key local venue for popular plays, ballets and other performances, while The Dome complex (page 46) or the Brighton Centre (page 42) will invariably be busy with gigs or sporting events.

The Pier is the main illuminated attraction of the seafront, open until late most summer nights, whilst nearby clubs and bars (below left) compete for attention with their own lighting displays. The huge glowing sign of The Komedia in Gardner Street, meanwhile (below right), draws people in for intimate gigs, comedy and cabaret nights and is a very popular spot.

Pavilion Lights

The Pavilion makes for one of the best evening sights in the city, strategically lit to enhance its exotic domes and minarets. In the 1970s, the lighting would slowly and dramatically change colour, creating atmospheric moods (as did the Old Steine fountains). Although now disappointingly static, the effect is still striking.

Lighting creates evocative shadows around the rear doorways and arches of the Pavilion and its gardens.

Christmas Spirit

Perhaps inevitably, Christmas is when the night time streets take on their most attractive appearance and the shops glow alluringly in the winter cold. The Lanes are particularly magical with their displays (main and inset), while the tree outside the Pier (right) stands strong against the bracing sea breezes.

The Clock Tower, decorated with a beautiful canopy of Christmas lights, seasonally enhancing its place as the centrepiece of a vibrant and unique city.

Epilogue

Sunset over Brighton, its place in the landscape revealed. As the only city in the county, and with its eclectic and go-ahead mix of inhabitants and key role as a holiday destination, Brighton is likely to remain an important part of the British cultural landscape too. These pages can only convey a little of the full Brightonian experience, but if all they achieve is to reinforce the place's specialness to its inhabitants, make ex-residents nostalgic or compel people from afar to want to visit, then they have served a purpose. Brighton will always be there for whoever wants to be part of it.